From Reflection to Resilience:
Navigating Life's Journey with Courage and Connection

RICARDO COSTA

ISBN: 9798320204048

DEDICATION

I dedicate this book to my mom. Without you nothing would have been possible.

My friends and family for the support, willingness to listen, talk and grow together.

TABLE OF CONTENTS

1
DON'T JUST MEET, TRULY UNDERSTAND: BUILDING DEEPER CONNECTIONS

In the hustle of our fast-paced lives, encounters often remain on the surface. We meet people, exchange pleasantries, but do we truly understand them? This chapter invites you to go beyond mere introductions, encouraging a journey into the depths of connection.

Introduction:

In a world bustling with interactions, the art of genuine connection can be overlooked. As we navigate through our daily routines, pausing to truly understand those we encounter can feel like a luxury we can't afford. Yet, it is precisely in these moments of pause that the magic of human connection unfolds.

Imagine for a moment a world where every interaction is imbued with meaning and understanding. Where conversations transcend small talk and delve into the essence of who we are. This is the world we aspire to create through the pages of this book—a world where connections are deepened, relationships flourish, and understanding abounds.

Asking the Right Questions:

Central to this exploration is the art of asking questions. Far too often, our interactions are limited to surface-level inquiries that barely scratch the surface of a person's being. "How are you?" we ask, without truly expecting—or perhaps even wanting—an honest answer.

But what if we dared to ask more? What if we delved into the stories behind the smiles, the dreams behind the laughter? What if we allowed others the space to share their joys, their sorrows, their hopes, and their fears?

Asking the right questions is the key to unlocking the door to deeper connections. It's about showing genuine interest in the lives of others and creating a space where they feel safe to open up and share. It's about listening not just with our ears, but with our hearts.

The Power of Empathy:

At the heart of genuine connection lies empathy—the ability to understand and share the feelings of another. Empathy is what allows us to truly connect with others on a deeper level, to see the world through their eyes, and to feel what they feel.

But empathy is more than just understanding—it's also about validation and acceptance. When we empathize with someone, we let them know that their feelings are valid, that they are seen and heard, and that they matter. This validation is a powerful catalyst for connection, fostering trust, and intimacy in our relationships.

Cultivating Curiosity:

Another essential ingredient in the recipe for deep connection is curiosity. Curiosity is what drives us to ask questions, to seek understanding, and to explore the unknown. It's what keeps conversations alive and vibrant, fueling our desire to learn more about the people we meet.

But curiosity is more than just asking questions—it's also about listening with an open mind and a genuine desire to learn. When we approach conversations with curiosity, we invite others to share their stories and perspectives, creating a space for connection to flourish.

The Importance of Vulnerability:

No discussion of deep connection would be complete without addressing the role of vulnerability. Vulnerability is the willingness to open ourselves up to others, to share our true thoughts, feelings, and experiences, even when it feels uncomfortable or risky.

While vulnerability can be scary, it is also incredibly powerful. When we allow ourselves to be vulnerable, we invite others to do the same, creating an atmosphere of trust and authenticity in our relationships. It's through vulnerability that true connection is forged, as we share our deepest selves with one another and find acceptance and understanding in return.

The Gift of Presence:

Finally, at the heart of deep connection lies the gift of presence. Presence is the act of being fully engaged and attentive in the moment, of giving our undivided attention to the person we are with. It's about putting aside distractions and truly being there for the people we care about.

In a world that is constantly vying for our attention, presence is a rare and precious gift. Yet, it is perhaps the most valuable thing we can offer in our relationships. When we are truly present with someone, we let them know that they are valued and important, that they have our full attention and support. And in doing so, we create a space for deep connection to flourish.

<u>Conclusion:</u>
As you embark on your journey to build deeper connections, remember that it is through asking the right questions, cultivating empathy and curiosity, embracing vulnerability, and offering the gift of presence that true connection is forged. It is in these moments of genuine connection that we find meaning, fulfillment, and joy in our relationships. So let us dare to be vulnerable, to ask the questions that truly matter, and to show up fully for the people we care about. For in the end, it is through connection that we find our truest selves and our greatest happiness.

2
EMBRACING THE ESSENCE OF TIME: A PRECIOUS RESOURCE

Time, the ever-elusive concept that governs our lives, holds a profound significance in our journey of self-discovery and connection. In this chapter, we delve into the essence of time, exploring its multifaceted role in shaping our experiences and relationships.

Introduction:

Time, the great equalizer, is a resource we all possess in limited supply. Yet, how we choose to spend our time speaks volumes about our priorities, values, and aspirations. In a world where busyness is glorified and productivity is paramount, it's easy to lose sight of the preciousness of each moment. But by embracing the essence of time, we can unlock its transformative power and cultivate a deeper sense of fulfillment in our lives.

Understanding Time:

To truly appreciate the value of time, we must first understand its nature and significance. Time is not merely a measure of minutes and hours—it's a currency of life, a finite resource that must be invested wisely. Each moment that passes is a gift, an opportunity to create, connect, and grow.

But time is also fleeting, ephemeral, slipping through our fingers like grains of sand. It's a reminder of our mortality, a call to seize the day and make the most of the time we have. As the ancient philosopher Seneca once said, "It's not that we have a short time to live, but that we waste a lot of it."

The Paradox of Time:

One of the greatest paradoxes of time is that while it is finite, it is also infinite in its possibilities. Each moment holds within it the potential for new beginnings, for growth, and for change. Yet, so often, we squander our time on trivial pursuits, distractions, and obligations that do not align with our true values and desires.

But it's never too late to reclaim our time, to realign our priorities, and to live with intention and purpose. By recognizing the preciousness of each moment and consciously choosing how we spend our time, we can unlock the full potential of our lives and create a legacy that endures beyond our years.

The Gift of Presence:

At the heart of embracing the essence of time lies the gift of presence—the act of being fully engaged and attentive in the moment. In a world that is constantly vying for our attention, presence is a rare and precious gift. Yet, it is perhaps the most valuable thing we can offer in our relationships.

When we are truly present with others, we show

them that they matter, that they have our full attention and support. We create a space for deep connection to flourish, for meaningful conversations to unfold, and for memories to be made. And in doing so, we honor the preciousness of each moment and the relationships that enrich our lives.

The Power of Mindfulness:

Mindfulness, the practice of being fully present and aware in the moment, is a powerful tool for embracing the essence of time. By cultivating mindfulness in our daily lives, we can learn to savor the moments, to appreciate the beauty and wonder of the world around us, and to live with gratitude and grace.

Mindfulness also allows us to let go of the past and the future, and to focus our attention on the present moment. It's a reminder that the only moment we truly have is now, and that it's up to us to make the most of it. As the Zen master Thich Nhat Hanh famously said, "The present moment is the only moment available to us, and it is the door to all moments."

<u>Conclusion:</u>

As you navigate the complexities of time in your journey of self-discovery and connection, remember that each moment is a precious gift, a chance to create, connect, and grow. By embracing the essence of time, cultivating presence and mindfulness, and living with intention and purpose, you can unlock the full potential of your life and create a legacy that endures beyond your years.

3
PHYSICAL TOUCH: SETTING BOUNDARIES AND INTERPRETING GESTURES

In the realm of human interaction, physical touch holds a unique significance. From a reassuring hand on the shoulder to an affectionate hug, touch has the power to convey emotions, establish connections, and foster intimacy. However, navigating the complexities of physical touch requires an understanding of boundaries, consent, and individual preferences.

Introduction:

Physical touch is a language unto itself—a silent communicator of emotions, intentions, and desires. Yet, despite its universal nature, the interpretation of touch can vary widely from person to person and culture to culture. In this chapter, we delve into the nuances of physical touch, exploring its role in our lives and the importance of setting boundaries and interpreting gestures with sensitivity and respect.

The Significance of Touch:

Touch is often referred to as the "language of the body," and for good reason. From the moment we are born, touch plays a crucial role in our development, fostering a sense of security, belonging, and connection. Studies have shown that physical touch releases oxytocin, often referred to as the "love hormone," which promotes bonding and reduces stress. Whether it's a comforting embrace from a loved one or a reassuring pat on the back from a colleague, touch has the power to convey care, support, and affection in ways that words alone cannot.

Understanding Boundaries:

While touch can be a powerful means of connection, it is essential to recognize and respect boundaries. Boundaries are the invisible lines that define the limits of acceptable touch for each individual. These boundaries are shaped by a variety of factors, including personal experiences, cultural norms, and individual preferences. What may be comfortable for one person may feel invasive or uncomfortable for another. Therefore, it is crucial to approach physical touch with sensitivity and to always ask for consent before initiating contact.

Navigating Consent:

Consent is the cornerstone of healthy touch. It is the explicit agreement between individuals to engage in physical contact, given freely and enthusiastically. Consent should never be assumed or coerced but should be actively sought and respected at all times. This means listening to verbal and nonverbal cues, respecting the other person's autonomy, and being prepared to accept a "no" without question or judgment. By prioritizing consent in our interactions, we create a culture of respect and safety where everyone feels empowered to express their boundaries and preferences.

Interpreting Gestures:

In addition to setting boundaries and seeking consent, it is essential to be mindful of how we interpret gestures of touch. What may be intended as a friendly gesture of affection or support may be perceived differently by the recipient, depending on their cultural background, personal history, or current emotional state. Therefore, it is important to approach touch with empathy and understanding, taking into account the other person's perspective and being sensitive to their comfort level.

Cultural Considerations:

Cultural norms and customs also play a significant role in shaping attitudes towards touch. In some cultures, physical affection is openly expressed and encouraged, while in others, it may be more reserved or restricted to specific contexts. It is essential to be aware of and respect cultural differences when navigating touch, recognizing that what may be acceptable in one culture may not be in another. By approaching touch with cultural sensitivity and openness, we can avoid misunderstandings and foster inclusive and respectful interactions.

Creating Safe Spaces:
Ultimately, the goal is to create safe and supportive spaces where individuals feel comfortable expressing their boundaries and preferences regarding touch. This requires ongoing communication, active listening, and a commitment to respecting the autonomy and agency of others. By prioritizing consent, empathy, and cultural sensitivity, we can cultivate environments where touch is experienced as a positive and affirming aspect of human connection.

Conclusion:
Physical touch is a fundamental aspect of human interaction, with the power to convey emotions, establish connections, and foster intimacy. By understanding and respecting boundaries, navigating consent, interpreting gestures with sensitivity, and embracing cultural diversity, we can create safe and supportive environments where touch is experienced as a positive and affirming aspect of human connection.

4
BEYOND TRANSACTIONS: UNVEILING THE STORIES OF PURSUIT IN MONEY AND PRESENTS

In our modern society, the pursuit of wealth and material possessions often takes center stage. From the latest gadgets to luxury cars, we are bombarded with messages that equate success and happiness with material abundance. However, beneath the surface of these transactions lie deeper narratives of values, aspirations, and the quest for fulfillment.

Introduction:
Money and presents are more than mere commodities—they are symbols of our desires, ambitions, and values. In this chapter, we delve into the stories behind the pursuit of wealth and material possessions, exploring the underlying motivations and the impact of these pursuits on our lives and relationships.

The Allure of Wealth:
For many, the pursuit of wealth is driven by a desire for security, status, and freedom. Whether it's the promise of financial independence, the thrill of success, or the admiration of others, wealth holds a

powerful allure that captivates and motivates. Yet, beneath the surface of this pursuit lies a deeper yearning for meaning and fulfillment—a quest for purpose that transcends material wealth alone.

The Role of Presents:

Similarly, the act of giving and receiving presents is laden with meaning and symbolism. Presents are not just tokens of affection or gratitude but reflections of our relationships, our values, and our understanding of the people we care about. Whether it's a thoughtful gesture of appreciation or an extravagant display of affection, presents speak volumes about our intentions and priorities.

Navigating Consumer Culture:

In a world dominated by consumer culture, it's easy to get swept up in the pursuit of more—more money, more possessions, more status. Yet, beneath the surface of this relentless pursuit lies a sense of emptiness and dissatisfaction—a nagging feeling that no amount of wealth or possessions can truly satisfy. This chapter encourages readers to pause and reflect on their own relationship with money and presents, challenging them to consider what truly brings meaning and fulfillment in their lives.

The Impact on Relationships:

The pursuit of wealth and material possessions can also have profound implications for our relationships. Whether it's the strain of financial stress, the tension of competing priorities, or the erosion of trust and intimacy, money can be a source of conflict and division in even the strongest of relationships. By exploring the stories behind these dynamics, readers gain insights into the complexities of balancing financial security with emotional well-being and the importance of open communication and shared values in navigating these challenges.

Finding Meaning Beyond Materialism:

Ultimately, the pursuit of wealth and material possessions is just one aspect of the human experience. True fulfillment lies not in the accumulation of possessions but in the richness of relationships, the depth of experiences, and the sense of purpose that comes from living in alignment with our values and passions. By shifting our focus from materialism to meaning, we can cultivate a more fulfilling and balanced approach to life—one that honors the stories behind the pursuit of wealth and presents while recognizing the inherent value of connection, creativity, and contribution.

<u>Conclusion:</u>

As we journey through the stories of pursuit in money and presents, we are reminded that wealth and possessions are but symbols of our deeper desires and aspirations. By exploring the narratives behind these pursuits, we gain insights into the complexities of human nature and the quest for meaning and fulfillment. In the end, it is not the wealth we amass or the presents we exchange that define us but the stories we tell and the connections we forge along the way.

5
JOURNEY OF DISCOVERY: UNRAVELING PREFERENCES IN TRAVEL AND TRANSPORTATION

Travel is not just about reaching a destination—it's about the journey itself, the experiences along the way, and the connections forged with people and places. In this chapter, we embark on a journey of exploration, uncovering the diverse preferences in travel and transportation that shape our adventures and define our experiences.

Introduction:

Travel is a universal human experience—a journey of discovery that broadens our horizons, challenges our assumptions, and enriches our lives in countless ways. Yet, within the realm of travel lie myriad preferences and choices that reflect our individual desires, priorities, and values. In this chapter, we delve into the nuances of travel and transportation, exploring the diverse ways in which we move through the world and the stories behind our journeys.

Modes of Transportation:

From planes and trains to automobiles and bicycles, the options for getting from point A to point B are as diverse as the destinations themselves. Each mode of transportation offers its own unique advantages and challenges, catering to different preferences and priorities. Whether it's the speed and convenience of air travel, the scenic beauty of train journeys, or the freedom and flexibility of road trips, our choice of transportation shapes our experiences and influences our perceptions of the places we visit.

Comfort and Convenience:

At the heart of our preferences in travel and transportation lie considerations of comfort and convenience. For some, the allure of first-class amenities and luxurious accommodations is irresistible, while others prioritize affordability and practicality. Similarly, the convenience of direct flights and express trains may appeal to those with tight schedules, while others prefer the leisurely pace of slower modes of transport. By exploring the stories behind these preferences, readers gain insights into the factors that shape our travel experiences and the trade-offs we make in pursuit of comfort and convenience.

Exploring Destinations:

Beyond the mode of transportation lies the destination itself—a tapestry of landscapes, cultures, and experiences waiting to be explored. Whether it's the bustling streets of a cosmopolitan city, the tranquil shores of a secluded beach, or the rugged beauty of a remote wilderness, each destination offers its own unique charms and opportunities for discovery. By delving into the stories behind our travel experiences, readers gain a deeper appreciation for the diversity of the world and the transformative power of exploration.

The Joy of Discovery:

At its core, travel is a journey of discovery—a voyage of self-discovery, cultural discovery, and discovery of the world around us. It's about stepping outside of our comfort zones, embracing the unknown, and opening ourselves up to new experiences and perspectives. By immersing ourselves in the stories of fellow travelers, we gain a deeper understanding of the universal human desire for connection, adventure, and growth.

Conclusion:

As we navigate the myriad preferences in travel and transportation, we are reminded that the journey itself is as important as the destination. Whether we're soaring through the skies, chugging along on a train, or cruising down the open road, each mode of transportation offers its own unique opportunities for discovery and connection. By embracing the diversity of travel experiences and the stories behind them, we enrich our own journeys and deepen our appreciation for the world around us.

6
NURTURING WELL-BEING: ESTABLISHING COMFORT AND UNDERSTANDING

Introduction:

In this section, we delve into the importance of nurturing personal well-being within relationships, emphasizing the significance of creating comfort and understanding. While maintaining the essence of a safe space, this chapter broadens its focus to encompass various aspects of fostering well-being within interpersonal dynamics.

Prioritizing Self-care:

At the heart of personal well-being lies the practice of self-care—a commitment to nurturing one's physical, emotional, and mental health. Beyond the daily grind, individuals must carve out time for activities that rejuvenate the soul. This might involve engaging in mindfulness practices, such as meditation or yoga, which promote inner peace and relaxation. Additionally, prioritizing regular exercise and maintaining healthy boundaries are essential components of self-care. By honoring one's needs and limitations, individuals can cultivate resilience and vitality, fostering a sense of inner harmony and fulfillment.

Mutual Respect and Boundaries:

Fundamental to healthy relationships is the cultivation of mutual respect and recognition of boundaries. Each person brings their unique experiences, preferences, and values to the table, and it's crucial to honor and validate each other's perspectives. Respecting each other's autonomy, preferences, and personal space fosters an atmosphere of trust and reciprocity, where individuals feel valued and supported in expressing their needs and desires. Clear communication and active listening play pivotal roles in establishing and maintaining these boundaries, ensuring that both parties feel heard and respected in the relationship.

Creating a Supportive Environment:

Beyond physical touch, fostering a supportive environment involves actively listening, validating, and empathizing with each other's experiences and emotions. Sometimes, all it takes is a listening ear or a comforting embrace to alleviate the weight of the world. By offering unwavering support and encouragement, partners can nurture emotional intimacy and deepen their connection, establishing a sense of safety and belonging. Creating rituals of connection, such as regular check-ins or shared activities, can further strengthen the bond between partners, fostering a sense of security and trust in the relationship.

Encouraging Personal Growth:

Healthy relationships provide a nurturing space for personal growth and self-expression, where individuals feel encouraged to pursue their passions, interests, and aspirations. Each person is on their unique journey of self-discovery and growth, and it's essential to celebrate and support each other's individuality. By celebrating each other's successes and aspirations, partners can cultivate a sense of empowerment and agency, fostering a relationship grounded in mutual respect and admiration. Encouraging personal development and pursuing shared goals can also strengthen the bond between partners, fostering a sense of partnership and camaraderie in the relationship.

Promoting Transparent Communication:

Effective communication is the cornerstone of healthy relationships, enabling partners to navigate challenges and foster intimacy with honesty and transparency. Open and honest communication creates a safe space for vulnerability and authenticity, allowing individuals to express their needs, concerns, and desires authentically. By fostering transparent communication, partners can deepen their understanding of each other and strengthen their emotional connection, resolving conflicts and building a stronger foundation for the relationship.

<u>Conclusion:</u>

In this section, we explore the multifaceted nature of nurturing personal well-being within relationships, emphasizing the importance of self-care, mutual respect, and transparent communication. By fostering an environment of comfort, understanding, and support, individuals can cultivate relationships that nurture their overall well-being, fostering a sense of fulfillment and connection that enriches their lives.

7
EXPECTATIONS OF HYGIENE: CULTIVATING COMFORT AND RESPECT IN PERSONAL CARE

Hygiene is not just a matter of cleanliness—it's a reflection of our values, preferences, and cultural norms. In this chapter, we delve into the nuances of personal hygiene, exploring the expectations, boundaries, and considerations that shape our practices and interactions.

Introduction:

Personal hygiene is a fundamental aspect of daily life—a routine that encompasses everything from bathing and grooming to skincare and dental care. Yet, beneath the surface of these practices lie deeper narratives of comfort, respect, and self-expression. In this chapter, we examine the expectations of hygiene, exploring the diverse ways in which individuals approach personal care and the importance of cultivating understanding and respect in these practices.

The Importance of Personal Hygiene:

Personal hygiene is essential not only for physical health but also for mental and emotional well-being. A clean and well-groomed appearance can boost confidence, enhance self-esteem, and create a positive impression on others. Conversely, poor hygiene can lead to discomfort, embarrassment, and social stigma. By prioritizing personal care, we not only maintain our physical health but also demonstrate respect for ourselves and those around us.

Cultural and Individual Variations:

Hygiene practices vary widely across cultures and individuals, reflecting diverse values, beliefs, and preferences. What may be considered acceptable in one culture may be frowned upon in another, highlighting the importance of cultural sensitivity and understanding. Similarly, individuals may have different standards and routines when it comes to personal care, influenced by factors such as upbringing, lifestyle, and personal preferences. By acknowledging and respecting these variations, we create an inclusive and respectful environment where everyone feels comfortable and accepted.

Navigating Expectations:

Navigating expectations of hygiene can be challenging, especially in social and professional settings where norms may be more rigidly defined. While it's important to adhere to basic standards of cleanliness and grooming, it's also essential to recognize and respect individual differences. What may seem like a minor deviation from the norm to one person may be a deeply ingrained aspect of identity or cultural practice for another. By approaching discussions of hygiene with empathy and understanding, we can foster open dialogue and create space for diverse perspectives to be heard and respected.

Addressing Sensitivities and Preferences:

In addition to cultural variations, individuals may also have sensitivities and preferences when it comes to hygiene products and practices. Allergies, skin conditions, and personal beliefs can all influence the products we use and the routines we follow. It's essential to be mindful of these sensitivities and preferences, respecting the choices of others and refraining from judgment or criticism. By creating an environment where individuals feel empowered to express their needs and preferences, we foster a culture of inclusivity and respect in personal care.

Promoting Health and Well-being:

Ultimately, the goal of personal hygiene is not just cleanliness but also health and well-being. By prioritizing hygiene practices that promote physical and mental wellness, we invest in our long-term health and happiness. This includes not only basic routines such as bathing and grooming but also practices that support overall wellness, such as regular exercise, nutritious eating, and stress management. By taking a holistic approach to personal care, we nurture our bodies, minds, and spirits, creating a foundation for a healthy and fulfilling life.

Conclusion:

As we navigate the expectations of hygiene, we are reminded of the importance of understanding, respect, and inclusivity in personal care practices. By acknowledging cultural and individual variations, navigating expectations with empathy and understanding, addressing sensitivities and preferences, and promoting health and well-being, we create a culture of comfort and respect in personal hygiene. In doing so, we not only maintain our physical health but also cultivate meaningful connections and foster a sense of belonging and acceptance in our communities.

8
EXPECTATIONS OF LEISURE AND FREE TIME: BALANCING ACTIVITIES AND REST

Leisure and free time are precious commodities in our busy lives, offering opportunities for relaxation, rejuvenation, and exploration. In this chapter, we explore the diverse expectations and preferences surrounding leisure activities, navigating the balance between active pursuits and restful moments.

Introduction:

Leisure and free time are essential for our overall well-being, providing opportunities to recharge, pursue hobbies, and connect with others. However, navigating the expectations of leisure activities can be complex, as individuals may have different preferences and priorities when it comes to how they spend their free time. In this chapter, we delve into the nuances of leisure and free time, exploring the expectations, boundaries, and considerations that shape our choices and experiences.

Active Pursuits vs. Restful Moments:

One of the central themes in discussions of leisure and free time is the balance between active pursuits and restful moments. Some individuals thrive on activity, seeking out opportunities for adventure, exploration, and social engagement. Others prefer quieter, more introspective activities, such as reading, meditation, or spending time alone in nature. By understanding and respecting these differences, we can create space for both active pursuits and restful moments in our lives, nurturing our physical, mental, and emotional well-being.

Exploring Personal Interests and Hobbies:

Leisure and free time provide opportunities for self-expression and personal growth through the pursuit of hobbies and interests. Whether it's playing a musical instrument, practicing a sport, or engaging in creative pursuits such as painting or writing, hobbies offer a sense of fulfillment and joy that transcends the demands of daily life. By exploring our interests and passions, we cultivate a sense of purpose and identity outside of work and obligations, enriching our lives and fostering a sense of fulfillment.

Social Expectations and Peer Pressure:

In addition to personal preferences, social expectations and peer pressure can also influence how we spend our leisure time. Whether it's the pressure to participate in social activities, attend events, or conform to certain cultural norms, external influences can shape our choices and experiences in significant ways. By being mindful of these influences and staying true to our own interests and values, we can navigate social expectations with authenticity and integrity, ensuring that our leisure time reflects our own priorities and preferences.

Setting Boundaries and Prioritizing Self-care:

Amidst the hustle and bustle of modern life, it's essential to set boundaries and prioritize self-care in our leisure and free time. This may involve saying no to activities that drain our energy or overwhelm our schedules, prioritizing activities that bring us joy and fulfillment, and carving out time for rest and relaxation. By honoring our own needs and limits, we can ensure that our leisure time is restorative, rejuvenating, and meaningful.

Embracing the Joy of Doing Nothing:

In a society that glorifies productivity and busyness, it's easy to overlook the simple pleasure of doing nothing—to savor moments of stillness and silence, to be present with ourselves and our surroundings, and to recharge our batteries without any agenda or expectations. By embracing the joy of doing nothing, we cultivate a deeper appreciation for the beauty of the present moment and the richness of life's simple pleasures.

Conclusion:

As we navigate the expectations of leisure and free time, we are reminded of the importance of balance, authenticity, and self-care in our pursuit of happiness and fulfillment. By honoring our own preferences and priorities, setting boundaries, and embracing the joy of both activity and rest, we create space for meaningful experiences and connections in our leisure time. In doing so, we nurture our physical, mental, and emotional well-being, fostering a sense of balance and harmony in our lives.

9
FOOD AND MEALS: NOURISHING BODY AND SOUL IN SHARED EXPERIENCES

Food is more than just sustenance—it's a catalyst for connection, a source of pleasure, and a reflection of culture and identity. In this chapter, we explore the diverse expectations and rituals surrounding food and meals, celebrating the joy of shared experiences and the bonds forged over shared meals.

Introduction:

Food holds a special place in our lives—it sustains us, nourishes us, and brings us together in shared experiences of joy and connection. From family dinners to holiday feasts, the rituals and traditions surrounding food and meals are deeply ingrained in our cultures and identities. In this chapter, we delve into the nuances of food and meals, exploring the diverse expectations, rituals, and considerations that shape our relationships with food and each other.

The Rituals of Mealtime:

Mealtime rituals are a cornerstone of human culture, providing opportunities for connection, conversation, and celebration. Whether it's the simple pleasure of sharing a meal with loved ones or the elaborate traditions of a holiday feast, the rituals of mealtime create a sense of belonging and community that transcends the act of eating alone. By honoring these rituals and traditions, we foster a sense of connection and continuity across generations and cultures.

The Language of Food:

Food is a universal language—a means of communication that transcends borders and barriers. The flavors, textures, and aromas of a meal speak volumes about our cultural heritage, personal preferences, and shared experiences. By exploring the diverse cuisines and culinary traditions of the world, we gain insights into the richness and diversity of human culture and the ways in which food shapes our identities and connections.

Navigating Dietary Preferences and Restrictions:

In today's multicultural and diverse society, navigating dietary preferences and restrictions is a common challenge. Whether it's due to health concerns, ethical beliefs, or cultural practices, individuals may have specific dietary needs and preferences that require accommodation and understanding. By respecting these preferences and offering inclusive options in our meal planning and preparation, we create an environment where everyone feels welcome and valued.

The Joy of Cooking and Sharing:

Cooking and sharing meals with others is a deeply rewarding experience that fosters connection, creativity, and collaboration. Whether it's gathering in the kitchen to prepare a meal together or sharing homemade dishes with friends and family, the act of cooking and sharing food creates lasting memories and strengthens bonds. By embracing the joy of cooking and sharing, we cultivate a sense of warmth and hospitality that nourishes both body and soul.

Navigating Food Costs and Responsibilities:

In addition to the joys of cooking and sharing, there are also practical considerations when it comes to food and meals, such as costs and responsibilities. Whether it's sharing the cost of groceries, dividing cooking duties, or coordinating meal planning, navigating these responsibilities requires open communication and mutual respect. By working together to address these practical concerns, we create a supportive and equitable environment where everyone can enjoy the benefits of shared meals.

Embracing the Joy of Food:

At its core, food is a source of joy—a pleasure to be savored, celebrated, and shared with others. Whether it's the simple pleasure of a home-cooked meal or the decadent indulgence of a special occasion feast, the joy of food lies in the connections and experiences it fosters. By embracing the joy of food and meals, we cultivate a deeper appreciation for the abundance and richness of life, savoring each moment and each bite with gratitude and delight.

Conclusion:

As we navigate the diverse expectations and rituals surrounding food and meals, we are reminded of the power of food to nourish both body and soul. By honoring mealtime rituals, exploring the language of food, respecting dietary preferences and restrictions, embracing the joy of cooking and sharing, and navigating food costs and responsibilities with care and consideration, we create a culture of connection and abundance in our shared experiences of food and meals.

10
THE ART OF CONVERSATION: CULTIVATING CONNECTION THROUGH COMMUNICATION

Conversation is the heartbeat of human connection—a dance of words, ideas, and emotions that binds us together in shared experiences of understanding and empathy. In this chapter, we explore the art of conversation, uncovering the nuances of communication and the power of dialogue to foster connection and growth.

Introduction:

Conversation is more than just an exchange of words—it's a dynamic interaction that shapes our relationships, influences our perceptions, and deepens our understanding of ourselves and others. In this chapter, we delve into the art of conversation, exploring the diverse elements that contribute to meaningful and enriching dialogue and the ways in which communication fosters connection and growth.

The Power of Listening:

At the heart of meaningful conversation lies the art of listening—the willingness to truly hear and understand the perspectives of others. Listening is not just about passively receiving information but actively engaging with others, offering empathy, validation, and support. By cultivating the skill of listening, we create space for genuine connection and empathy to flourish, fostering deeper relationships and mutual understanding.

The Importance of Authenticity:

Authenticity is the cornerstone of effective communication—it's about speaking from the heart, expressing our true thoughts and feelings, and being open and honest with ourselves and others. Authentic conversation requires vulnerability and courage, as we share our joys, fears, and vulnerabilities with those around us. By embracing authenticity in our interactions, we create an environment where trust and intimacy can thrive, fostering deeper connections and mutual respect.

Navigating Difficult Conversations:

While conversation has the power to foster connection and understanding, it can also be challenging, especially when addressing difficult topics or navigating conflict. In these moments, it's essential to approach conversation with empathy, curiosity, and a willingness to listen and learn from others. By engaging in open and honest dialogue, we create opportunities for growth and reconciliation, transforming conflict into opportunities for deeper understanding and connection.

Cultivating Curiosity and Empathy:

Curiosity and empathy are essential qualities in effective communication—they enable us to approach conversation with an open mind and a compassionate heart, seeking to understand the perspectives and experiences of others. By cultivating curiosity and empathy, we create space for diverse voices to be heard and valued, fostering a culture of inclusion and respect in our interactions.

The Art of Asking Questions:

Asking questions is a powerful tool in conversation—it invites others to share their thoughts, feelings, and experiences, creating opportunities for connection and discovery. By asking open-ended questions and actively listening to the responses, we demonstrate curiosity and engagement, fostering meaningful dialogue and deepening our connections with others.

Embracing Silence and Reflection:

In the midst of conversation, there is also value in silence and reflection—moments of pause that allow us to process our thoughts and emotions, integrate new information, and deepen our understanding of ourselves and others. By embracing silence and reflection in our interactions, we create space for introspection and growth, fostering deeper connections and a greater sense of presence and authenticity.

<u>Conclusion:</u>

As we explore the art of conversation, we are reminded of its power to foster connection, understanding, and growth. By embracing the qualities of listening, authenticity, curiosity, and empathy, we create space for meaningful dialogue and deeper relationships to flourish. In doing so, we cultivate a culture of connection and mutual respect, enriching our lives and the lives of those around us through the power of communication.

11

THE POWER OF SPORTS: BUILDING COMMUNITY AND CONNECTION THROUGH PHYSICAL ACTIVITY

Sports are more than just games—they're a universal language that transcends borders, cultures, and backgrounds, uniting individuals in shared experiences of teamwork, competition, and camaraderie. In this chapter, we explore the power of sports to build community and connection, celebrating the ways in which physical activity fosters personal growth, social cohesion, and collective well-being.

Introduction:

Sports have long served as a powerful force for bringing people together, fostering connections, and promoting physical and mental well-being. Whether it's the thrill of competition, the camaraderie of teamwork, or the joy of physical activity, sports offer a myriad of benefits that extend far beyond the playing field. In this chapter, we delve into the power of sports to build community and connection, exploring the ways in which physical activity enriches our lives and strengthens our bonds with others.

The Thrill of Competition:

At the heart of sports lies the thrill of competition—a chance to test our skills, push our limits, and strive for excellence. Whether it's a friendly game of pick-up basketball or the intensity of professional athletics, competition fuels our passion for sports and drives us to achieve our best. Yet, competition is not just about winning or losing—it's about the journey of self-discovery, personal growth, and resilience that unfolds along the way.

The Camaraderie of Teamwork:

Team sports offer a unique opportunity for connection and camaraderie, as individuals come together to work towards a common goal. Through teamwork, athletes learn the value of collaboration, communication, and trust, forging bonds that extend beyond the playing field. Whether it's the shared triumph of victory or the collective support in times of defeat, team sports foster a sense of belonging and unity that strengthens communities and enriches lives.

Physical Activity and Well-being:

Beyond the competitive arena, sports and physical activity play a crucial role in promoting physical and mental well-being. Regular exercise has been shown to reduce the risk of chronic disease, improve mood and mental health, and enhance overall quality of life. Whether it's a leisurely jog in the park, a challenging hike in the mountains, or a lively game of soccer with friends, physical activity offers a myriad of benefits that nourish body, mind, and spirit.

Inclusivity and Diversity:

One of the most powerful aspects of sports is their ability to bring together individuals from diverse backgrounds and experiences, fostering inclusivity and unity. Regardless of age, gender, race, or ability, sports offer a level playing field where everyone has the opportunity to participate, contribute, and succeed. By embracing diversity and celebrating the unique talents and perspectives of each individual, sports create a sense of belonging and acceptance that transcends differences and unites us in common purpose.

Community Building and Social Cohesion:

Sports have the power to strengthen communities and promote social cohesion, as individuals come together to support and celebrate shared interests and achievements. Whether it's a local sports team, a community fitness program, or a city-wide event, sports provide opportunities for connection, celebration, and collective action. By fostering a sense of pride and belonging, sports contribute to the fabric of society, enriching lives and strengthening bonds within and across communities.

Empowering Youth and Inspiring Future Generations:

For many young people, sports serve as a gateway to personal growth, self-confidence, and leadership development. Through participation in sports, children and adolescents learn valuable life skills such as teamwork, resilience, and goal-setting, setting the stage for success both on and off the playing field. By investing in youth sports programs and providing access to quality coaching and resources, communities can empower young people to reach their full potential and become leaders of tomorrow.

Conclusion:

As we celebrate the power of sports to build community and connection, we are reminded of their profound impact on our lives and societies. Whether it's the thrill of competition, the camaraderie of teamwork, or the joy of physical activity, sports enrich our lives in countless ways, fostering personal growth, social cohesion, and collective well-being. By embracing the values of inclusivity, diversity, and community building that sports represent, we can create a world where everyone has the opportunity to participate, belong, and thrive.

12
NAVIGATING STRESS: HARNESSING PRESSURE AS A CATALYST FOR GROWTH AND RESILIENCE

Stress is an inevitable part of life—a natural response to the challenges and uncertainties we face on a daily basis. In this chapter, we explore the complexities of stress, offering strategies for navigating pressure and harnessing its transformative potential as a catalyst for growth and resilience.

Introduction:

Stress is a universal experience—an unavoidable aspect of human existence that manifests in response to the demands and pressures of daily life. While stress can be overwhelming and debilitating, it can also serve as a powerful catalyst for growth and resilience, pushing us to adapt, evolve, and thrive in the face of adversity. In this chapter, we delve into the complexities of stress, exploring its impact on our lives and offering strategies for navigating pressure with grace and resilience.

Understanding Stress:

At its core, stress is a physiological response to perceived threats or challenges—a survival mechanism that mobilizes our bodies and minds to cope with danger or discomfort. While acute stress can be beneficial, helping us to focus, perform, and overcome obstacles, chronic stress can have detrimental effects on our physical, mental, and emotional well-being. By understanding the mechanisms of stress and its impact on our bodies and minds, we can better navigate its challenges and harness its potential for growth.

Identifying Triggers and Patterns:

One of the first steps in navigating stress is identifying its triggers and patterns—the situations, thoughts, and behaviors that contribute to feelings of pressure and overwhelm. By recognizing the signs of stress and understanding its underlying causes, we can take proactive steps to manage our responses and mitigate its impact on our lives. This may involve setting boundaries, practicing self-care, and seeking support from friends, family, or mental health professionals.

Cultivating Resilience:

Resilience is the ability to bounce back from adversity—to adapt, grow, and thrive in the face of challenges. While resilience is often seen as a trait that some individuals possess innately, it is also a skill that can be cultivated and strengthened over time. By developing coping strategies, fostering positive thinking, and building a support network of friends, family, and mentors, we can enhance our resilience and navigate stress with greater ease and grace.

Embracing Mindfulness and Self-compassion:

Mindfulness and self-compassion are powerful tools for navigating stress, enabling us to stay present, grounded, and compassionate towards ourselves and others. Mindfulness practices such as meditation, deep breathing, and body scans can help to calm the mind, reduce anxiety, and cultivate a sense of inner peace and resilience. Similarly, self-compassion involves treating ourselves with kindness and understanding, especially in times of difficulty or failure. By embracing mindfulness and self-compassion, we can cultivate a sense of inner strength and resilience that helps us weather life's storms with grace and resilience.

Seeking Support and Connection:

In times of stress, it's essential to reach out for support and connection from others. Whether it's talking to a trusted friend, seeking guidance from a mentor, or attending a support group, sharing our experiences and feelings with others can provide comfort, validation, and perspective. By fostering connections with others and building a supportive network of relationships, we create a sense of belonging and community that strengthens our resilience and enhances our ability to cope with stress.

Finding Meaning and Purpose:

Stress can be an opportunity for growth and self-discovery—a catalyst for clarifying our values, priorities, and goals in life. By reframing stress as a challenge to be embraced rather than a problem to be avoided, we can find meaning and purpose in our experiences, channeling our energy and focus towards pursuits that align with our deepest passions and aspirations. Whether it's pursuing a new career path, embarking on a creative project, or deepening our relationships with loved ones, stress can serve as a catalyst for positive change and personal growth.

Conclusion:

As we navigate the complexities of stress, we are reminded of its transformative potential as a catalyst for growth and resilience. By understanding the mechanisms of stress, identifying its triggers and patterns, cultivating resilience through mindfulness and self-compassion, seeking support and connection from others, and finding meaning and purpose in our experiences, we can navigate pressure with grace and resilience, emerging stronger, wiser, and more resilient than before.

13
THE JOURNEY CONTINUES: EMBRACING GROWTH AND TRANSFORMATION

Life is a journey—an ongoing process of growth, discovery, and transformation that unfolds with each passing moment. In this final chapter, we reflect on the lessons learned, the challenges overcome, and the wisdom gained along the way, embracing the journey of self-discovery and personal evolution.

Introduction:

As we reach the end of this book, we pause to reflect on the journey we've undertaken together—a journey of self-discovery, personal growth, and empowerment. Along the way, we've explored the depths of our hearts and minds, confronted our fears and insecurities, and embraced the beauty and complexity of the human experience. In this final chapter, we celebrate the wisdom gained, the connections forged, and the transformations experienced, as we continue to navigate the ever-unfolding journey of life.

Embracing Change and Uncertainty:

Life is inherently uncertain—a continuous cycle of change and adaptation that challenges us to evolve and grow. While change can be unsettling and uncomfortable, it also holds the promise of new opportunities, experiences, and perspectives. By embracing change with courage and resilience, we open ourselves up to the possibilities that lie beyond our comfort zones, trusting in our ability to navigate the unknown with grace and determination.

Cultivating Gratitude and Appreciation:

Amidst the challenges and uncertainties of life, it's essential to cultivate gratitude and appreciation for the blessings and abundance that surround us. Gratitude is a powerful practice that shifts our focus from scarcity to abundance, from fear to love, reminding us of the beauty and richness of life's gifts, both big and small. By cultivating gratitude in our hearts and minds, we invite more joy, fulfillment, and connection into our lives, fostering a sense of contentment and peace amidst life's ups and downs.

Honoring the Journey of Self-discovery:

The journey of self-discovery is an ongoing process of exploration and introspection—a quest to uncover the depths of our true selves and embrace our authentic essence. Along the way, we encounter obstacles, setbacks, and moments of doubt, but we also discover our strengths, passions, and innermost desires. By honoring the journey of self-discovery with curiosity and compassion, we reclaim our power, align with our purpose, and create lives of meaning and fulfillment.

Celebrating Growth and Resilience:

Throughout life's journey, we encounter countless challenges and obstacles that test our resilience and strength. Yet, with each challenge overcome, we emerge stronger, wiser, and more resilient than before. By celebrating our growth and resilience, we acknowledge the lessons learned, the obstacles overcome, and the victories achieved along the way. We recognize the courage and determination that reside within us, empowering us to face whatever challenges may come with grace and fortitude.

Nurturing Connections and Relationships:

At the heart of life's journey lies the connections and relationships we forge along the way. Whether it's the bonds of family, the friendships of kindred spirits, or the love of romantic partners, relationships enrich our lives with meaning, joy, and companionship. By nurturing connections with others, we create a support network of love and encouragement that sustains us through life's trials and triumphs, reminding us that we are never alone on this journey.

<u>Embracing the Unknown with Faith and Trust:</u>
As we continue along life's journey, we encounter the unknown—the mysteries and uncertainties that lie beyond our understanding. In these moments, it's essential to cultivate faith and trust in the wisdom of the universe, knowing that we are guided and supported every step of the way. By surrendering to the flow of life with faith and trust, we open ourselves up to infinite possibilities and opportunities for growth, knowing that the journey ahead is filled with endless potential and promise.

<u>Conclusion:</u>
As we conclude this book and reflect on the journey we've shared, we are reminded of the beauty and complexity of the human experience. Life is a journey—a sacred pilgrimage of self-discovery, growth, and transformation that unfolds with each passing moment. Along the way, we encounter joys and sorrows, triumphs and challenges, but through it all, we remain steadfast in our commitment to embrace the journey with open hearts and minds. May we continue to navigate life's twists and turns with courage, grace, and resilience, knowing that the journey of self-discovery and personal evolution is a lifelong adventure filled with endless possibilities and opportunities for growth.

14
THE POWER OF REFLECTION: CULTIVATING WISDOM THROUGH SELF-EXAMINATION

Introduction:

Reflection is a powerful tool for personal growth and development, offering us the opportunity to pause, assess, and learn from our experiences. In this chapter, we explore the importance of reflection in cultivating wisdom and insight, as well as practical strategies for incorporating reflection into our daily lives.

The Practice of Reflection:

Reflection involves taking the time to consciously examine our thoughts, feelings, and actions, with the goal of gaining insight and understanding. This may involve journaling, meditation, or simply quiet contemplation. By regularly engaging in the practice of reflection, we deepen our self-awareness, identify patterns and habits, and gain clarity about our values and goals.

Learning from Mistakes:

One of the most powerful aspects of reflection is its ability to help us learn from our mistakes. By honestly examining our failures and setbacks, we uncover valuable lessons and insights that can inform our future actions and decisions. Rather than dwelling on our mistakes with regret or shame, we can use reflection as a tool for growth and self-improvement.

Cultivating Gratitude:

Reflection also allows us to cultivate gratitude for the blessings and abundance in our lives. By taking the time to acknowledge and appreciate the positive aspects of our experiences, we foster a sense of contentment and fulfillment. Gratitude has been shown to improve mental health, enhance relationships, and increase resilience in the face of adversity.

Setting Intentions:

Reflection can also help us set intentions for the future, clarifying our values and goals and aligning our actions with our aspirations. By reflecting on our past experiences and considering what we want to create in our lives, we can set meaningful intentions that guide our behavior and choices moving forward.

<u>Embracing Self-Compassion:</u>

Finally, reflection provides an opportunity to practice self-compassion—to treat ourselves with kindness and understanding, especially in moments of difficulty or failure. By acknowledging our humanity and accepting ourselves as imperfect beings, we create space for growth and transformation without judgment or self-criticism.

<u>Conclusion:</u>

As we conclude this chapter on the power of reflection, we are reminded of its profound impact on our lives and well-being. By regularly engaging in the practice of reflection, we deepen our self-awareness, learn from our experiences, and cultivate wisdom and insight. Whether through journaling, meditation, or quiet contemplation, reflection offers us a pathway to personal growth, resilience, and fulfillment.

15
THE JOURNEY WITHIN: EMBRACING GROWTH, CONNECTION, AND RESILIENCE

Introduction:

As we conclude our journey together, we pause to reflect on the wisdom gained, the connections forged, and the transformations experienced along the way. From exploring the depths of self-discovery to embracing the power of connection and resilience, each chapter has been a stepping stone on the path to personal growth and empowerment. In this final chapter, we wrap up our exploration by celebrating the journey within—a journey of courage, compassion, and self-discovery that continues to unfold with each passing moment.

Reflecting on Our Journey:

Our journey began with an exploration of the self—the intricacies of our identities, values, and aspirations. Through reflection, introspection, and self-examination, we uncovered the depths of our true selves, embracing authenticity and vulnerability as we navigated the complexities of the human experience. Along the way, we encountered challenges and obstacles that tested our resilience and strength, but we emerged stronger, wiser, and more empowered than before.

Building Connections and Community:

Central to our journey has been the power of connection and community—the bonds of friendship, family, and shared experiences that sustain us through life's ups and downs. From the camaraderie of teamwork to the support of loved ones, we discovered the profound impact of relationships in shaping our sense of belonging and identity. Through empathy, compassion, and mutual respect, we forged connections that enriched our lives and strengthened our resilience in the face of adversity.

Navigating Life's Challenges with Grace and Resilience:

Life is full of challenges and uncertainties, but it is also ripe with opportunities for growth and transformation. By embracing change with courage and resilience, we navigated life's twists and turns with grace and determination, trusting in our ability to overcome obstacles and emerge stronger on the other side. Whether facing the pressures of stress, the complexities of relationships, or the uncertainties of the future, we met each challenge with courage, compassion, and a steadfast belief in our own resilience.

<u>Embracing Gratitude and Joy:</u>
Amidst life's challenges and uncertainties, we cultivated gratitude and joy for the blessings and abundance that surround us. Through mindfulness, reflection, and appreciation, we learned to savor life's simple pleasures, finding beauty and meaning in the present moment. By embracing gratitude and joy as guiding principles in our lives, we fostered a sense of contentment and fulfillment that transcended circumstances, anchoring us in the richness and abundance of the here and now.

<u>Looking Ahead with Hope and Optimism:</u>
As we conclude our journey, we look ahead with hope and optimism, embracing the possibilities and opportunities that lie on the horizon. With the wisdom gained from our experiences, the connections forged with others, and the resilience cultivated within ourselves, we embark on the next chapter of our lives with confidence and purpose. Though the road ahead may be uncertain, we journey forward with open hearts and minds, knowing that the journey within is an ever-unfolding adventure filled with endless opportunities for growth, connection, and transformation.

Conclusion:

As we bid farewell to this journey, we are reminded that the journey within is ongoing—a continuous process of growth, discovery, and self-transformation that extends far beyond the pages of this book. Though our paths may diverge, we carry with us the lessons learned, the connections forged, and the wisdom gained, as we continue to navigate the complexities of the human experience with courage, compassion, and resilience. May we embrace each moment with gratitude and joy, knowing that the journey within is a sacred pilgrimage of self-discovery and empowerment that enriches our lives and uplifts the world around us.